TIME
FOR KIDS
READERS

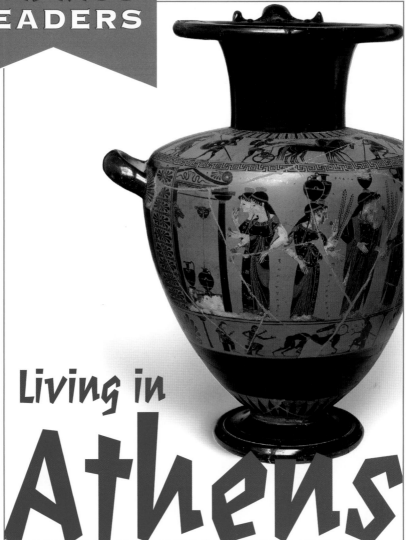

Living in
Athens

by Lisa Trumbauer

 Harcourt

Orlando   Austin   Chicago   New York   Toronto   London   San Diego

Visit *The Learning Site!*
www.harcourtschool.com

Athens is a city in Greece. Greece is a country on the continent of Europe. This is what Athens looks like today.

GREECE

Athens

Aegean Sea

ALBANIA

MACEDONIA

TURKEY

Sea of Crete

Crete

ATLANTIC OCEAN

EUROPE

GREECE

Today more than three million people live in Athens, Greece.

Athens is a very old city. You can still see some of its buildings from long ago. The Parthenon was a temple built on a hill above Athens. It was built about 2,500 years ago.

The Parthenon was built on the highest point in Athens, called the Acropolis.

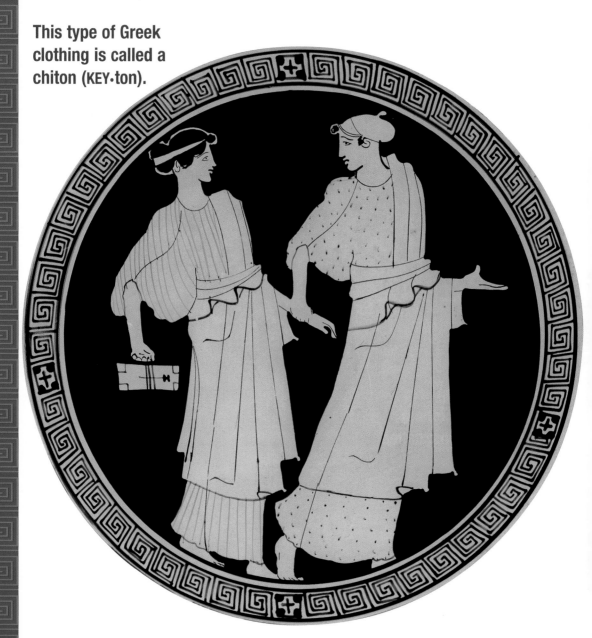

Your life would be very different if you lived thousands of years ago in ancient Greece. Your clothing would be different, too. People in ancient Greece wore loose clothing.

4

Boys went to school until they were about 14 or 15 years old. Girls did not go to school at all.

Children in ancient Greece played games, just like children today.

If you lived in Greece long ago, you would probably hear a lot of music. People played music and sang songs for special times.

In ancient Greece, musicians played a stringed instrumemt called a lyre (LIE·er).

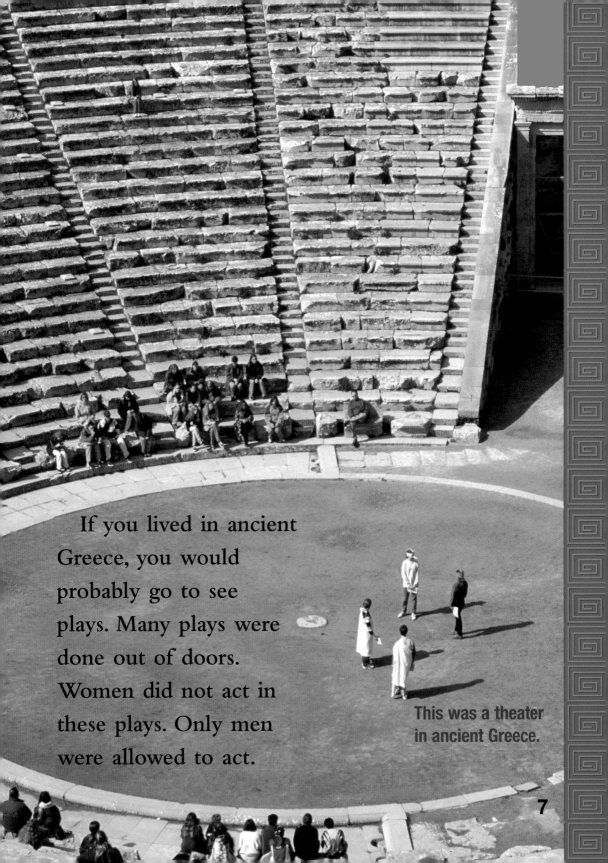

If you lived in ancient Greece, you would probably go to see plays. Many plays were done out of doors. Women did not act in these plays. Only men were allowed to act.

This was a theater in ancient Greece.

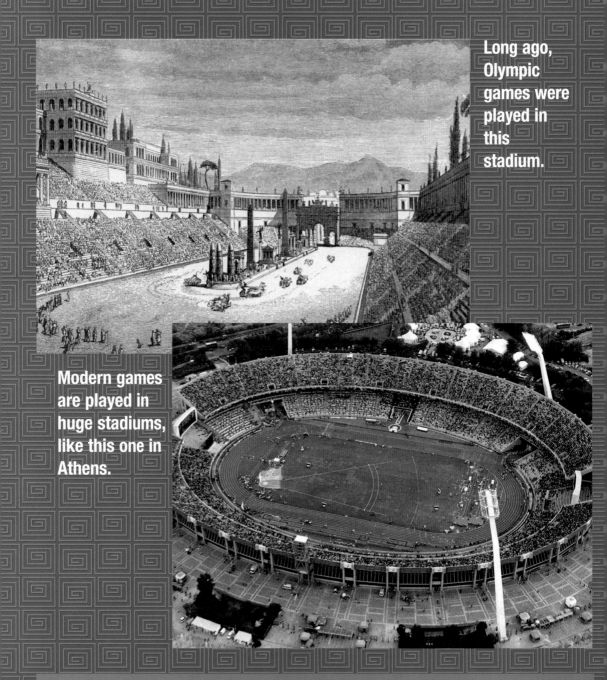

Long ago, Olympic games were played in this stadium.

Modern games are played in huge stadiums, like this one in Athens.

Sports were important, too. The Olympics started in ancient Greece. Some of our stadiums look like the sports stadiums of ancient Greece.

8